What People Are Saying About
TALES FROM BEHIND THE WHEEL: YEAR ONE

"After reading this book, I'm tempted to become a rideshare driver myself just to have some great stories to tell. Jonathan Wong gives us a true insider's look into life as a rideshare driver, from giving rides to crazy and rude people as well as celebrities and professionals to sharing some very human moments when he can make a passenger's life a little better or get someone home safely. You'll never look at your Uber driver in the same way after reading Tales from Behind the Wheel: Year One."

— Tyler R. Tichelaar, Ph.D. and Award-Winning Author of *Narrow Lives* and *The Best Place*

"Fun true stories that place you, the reader, in the driver's seat, and help you see life from a different perspective."

— Susan Friedmann, CSP, International Bestselling Author of *Riches in Niches: How to Make it BIG in a small Market*

"While I enjoyed the funny stories like everyone else, I was most impressed with the insight into the world of rideshare drivers. They really do 'keep the town moving' each and every day, whether they are taking people to work, school, home, on errands or taking tourists to attractions. With that comes all the stories you can expect—especially those at the deep human level. A fascinating, funny, and heart-warming read."

— Justine Gronwald, Author of *LAWYER UP!: 7 Step Guide to Help You Find the Right Attorney for YOUR Needs*

"Jonathan blows me away with his diversity. One minute he's writing a book about succeeding in college and the next he's making me laugh with a book about ridesharing. His ability to seemlessly move between two very different subjects successfully makes my mind spin! This book is a fun, easy read that really makes me appreciate both Jonathan's diversity and the diversity of the riders he picks up. If only I was a fly on the wall in his car...what fun I'd have!"

— Nicole Gabriel, Author of *Healing Your Dog Naturally*

"Wong provides a very fascinating look into the world of ride-share. I was actually quite surprised at the variety of people who commute via Uber or Lyft on a daily basis. Indeed, it is a true slice of life! The stories are funny but also very endearing. Timeless."

— Patti Mulry, Author of *When Hope Shows Up: Transforming Your Body, Health, and Mind to Create an Extraordinary Life*

"I literally felt like I was in the passenger's seat going along for a ride with Jonathan through the streets of Honolulu. The stories were funny and easy to read! Highly recommended!"

— Nora Yolles-Young, Author of *Healing Effortlessly*

"Such an interesting read! I had no idea just how diverse a group of people Uber and Lyft drivers chauffeur around every day! The stories are funny and entertaining and in some cases quite educational! You'll definitely want to read this!"

— Kapono Kobylanski, Author of *Waking Up: With No Excuses*

"This book has a great balance and mix of laugh out loud moments and heart-warming stories. You'll never look at your Uber or Lyft driver the same again."

— Heather Howell, Author of *Dream It, See It, Be It*

"You'll be laughing the whole time while learning something useful. If you've ever thought of driving for Uber or Lyft, this is a must-read. You'll see what life is like as a rideshare driver."

— *Natalie Kawai, Author of Conversations with Mother Goddess*

"I want to drive for Uber and Lyft now! Wow!"

— Laurie Bethell, Professional Holistic Health Coach, Certified Transformational Breath Facilitator, Author of *Bear Witness: Striving to Live Each Moment Like It Is Your Last*

"This book is a true tour-de-force through the human experience from cruising it out with partiers and drunks on the weekends, dealing with angry cab drivers, taking tourists around town, or even the mundane activity of taking folks to work each day. The book is a fun and short read and the stories and lessons are timeless. Highly recommended!"

— Susan Ortolano, M.A., Relationship Coach &
Author of *Remarrying Right*

"Because I grew up in Honolulu, I loved these stories! It's always cool to see your hometown through a new lens. What a perfect way to earn some extra cash while working toward your dream and have some fun along the way!"

— Jeffery Bow, Coach, Speaker, and Author of
*Stop Thinking, Start Believing: How to
Break Through Fear and Ignite Your Brilliance*

"If you were ever a fan of shows like Taxi Cab Confessions, you'll love Jonathan Wong's Tales from Behind the Wheel. Containing everything from stories of driving drunks, savvy business travelers, tourists, frustrated strippers, the everyday going to work, bad GPS directions, and dealing with angry cab drivers and traffic cops, it'll make you'll laugh, shake your head, and go, "Oh wow!" You'll look at your Uber driver differently the next time you take a ride."

— Brodi Goshi, Co-Founder, iConnectUHI

TALES FROM BEHIND THE WHEEL

YEAR ONE

55 OUTRAGEOUS, CRAZY, FUNNY, MUNDANE, AND TRUE STORIES FROM A RIDESHARE DRIVER IN PARADISE

JONATHAN WONG

FOREWORD BY LOPAKA KAPANUI

AVIVA PUBLISHING
New York

Tales From Behind the Wheel: Year One
55 Outrageous, Crazy, Funny, Mundane, and True Stories from a Rideshare Driver in Paradise

Copyright © 2017 by Jonathan Wong

All Rights Reserved. No part of this book may be used or reproduced in any manner whatsoever without the expressed written consent of the author, except in the case of brief quotations with credit embodied in articles, books, and reviews.

Address all inquiries to:
Jonathan Wong
P.O. Box 23259
Honolulu, HI 96823
(213) 262-9570
www.TalesFromBehindTheWheel.com

ISBN: 978-1-9443350-1-4
Library of Congress Control Number: 2016918808

Editor: Tyler Tichelaar, Superior Book Productions
Cover and Interior Design: Nicole Gabriel, AngelDog Productions

Published by:
Aviva Publishing
Lake Placid, NY
(518) 523-1320
www.avivapubs.com

Every attempt has been made to source properly all quotes.

Printed in the USA
First Edition

For additional copies visit:
www.TalesFromBehindTheWheel.com

DEDICATION

To my friends and colleagues in the Rideshare808 Group on Facebook for your camaraderie, your ability to make frustrating moments bearable, and all the funny stories we've shared. You helped make an initially isolating job feel just like a workplace with colleagues I'd be in contact with every day. I've enjoyed hearing your individual "Tales from Behind the Wheel" over the past year.

To my parents, Allen and Charlotte, and my brother Mike and sister-in-law Maureen for supporting me and loving me through it all.

To my former colleagues in the English Departments at the University of Hawaii Community Colleges, especially Reid and Brenda, who meant so much to me personally during those years, and to Brenda, Eric, and Lisa, alongside whom I'm glad to say I'm now a published author.

And most importantly, to Liane, who waits patiently for me to come home every time I go on the road. I love you more than you'll ever truly know.

ACKNOWLEDGMENTS

A big mahalo (thank you) to the following individuals without whom this book would not have been possible.

To Patrick Snow, the greatest book publishing and marketing coach on the planet who taught me and helped me to realize my dreams of becoming a published author.

To Nicole Gabriel, for the most beautiful book covers on the planet.

To Tyler Tichelaar, who makes me sound far more eloquent than I actually am.

To Brodi Goshi, Justine Gronwald, Jodi Uehara, and John Noland, who helped support and promote my rideshare ventures at the outset.

CONTENTS

Foreword by Lopaka Kapanui	15
Introduction: We All Love Stories	19
Chapter 1: Freaks Come Out at Night	23
Chapter 2: Here on Business	45
Chapter 3: Celebrity Sightings	57
Chapter 4: The Everyday Rider	67
Chapter 5: Cab Wars	77
Chapter 6: #GPSFails	87
Chapter 7: "I'm Sorry, Officer."	97
Chapter 8: "I'm Here. Where Are You?"	109
Chapter 9: The Virtual Water Cooler	117
A Final Note	121
Appendices	
Appendix A: Rideshare Etiquette	129

Appendix B: New Rider and Driver Offer	135
Appendix C: Driving Profits Offer	141
Appendix D: Turo and Airbnb Offer	145
About the Author	149
Akamai Visionary Consulting	153
Jonathan Speaks	155
Succeeding In College and Life	159

FOREWORD

As storytellers, we are keepers of people, place, and time. Being a professional storyteller is a *kuleana* (responsibility) I accept and take very seriously. Through our work as storytellers, we preserve and pass on knowledge and traditions. While many find entertainment in our stories, we also teach valuable lessons to others so we can be better people.

As long as I have known Jonathan Wong, he has always been a hard worker who was always in the middle of things. Even when he contacted me years ago to share stories with his students and colleagues at the community college, it was obvious that he was the behind-the-scenes guy who greased the squeaky wheel. Jonathan has been successful in everything he's done, and if you don't believe me, you should take a look at the three master's degrees he has under his belt. Jonathan has been through hard times as well, but even during those adverse events, he has never stopped moving forward, so I am honored to write this foreword for his new book.

TALES FROM BEHIND THE WHEEL

It's always been said that everyone has a story to tell, and that is true. However, not everyone can *tell* a story. In this book, you will meet someone who can not only tell a story, but someone who can transport you into it, as if you were there yourself. Equally entertaining and insightful, these tales will make you laugh just as much as shake your head or say, "Oh, wow, I never knew that" as you journey through the streets of Honolulu with Jonathan as your personal Uber and Lyft driver. Entertaining and insightful—those are always the hallmarks of a great storyteller. Such is Jonathan Wong.

Lopaka Kapanui

Owner, Mysteries of Hawaii
Best-Selling Author of *Haunted Hawaiian Nights, The Legend of Morgan's Corner and Other Ghost Stories of Hawaii,* and *Mysteries of Honolulu*

http://mysteries-of-hawaii.com/

INTRODUCTION
WE ALL LOVE STORIES

We all love stories and to be entertained. Whether it's to laugh or to learn a valuable life lesson, stories are what life is made of. We laugh at life's little moments. We're shocked. We shake our heads. We relate to each other through the stories we share. We also look deeper into the stories we share at the life lessons and teachable moments that they present to us.

I've spent my life as a teacher. I taught college for many years. I performed as an improv comedian for several years, and I dabbled in stand-up comedy. In my current life, I lead seminars and workshops and speak before groups who wish to hear and learn what I have to share.

In this book, *Tales from Behind the Wheel: Year One*, I collect and share my funniest, strangest, truest, and best stories of my

TALES FROM BEHIND THE WHEEL

first year as a rideshare driver for Uber and Lyft. I hope you'll find them entertaining. I hope you learn a little something useful that you didn't know before. I hope you will laugh with me at the funny strange, funny true, and outright hilarious moments. I hope you shake, you vent, or you pull your hair during the frustrating moments. I hope you'll nod in agreement during the moments when you learn or see life's truths in the tales I share, for ultimately, we are all everyday people, whether we're simply on our way to work, to school, or are taking a trip for business or pleasure in a far-off land. The human experience is the same no matter where we are or what we do. And part of the marvel and pleasure in creating tales is the privilege to touch others' lives on this shared journey through life. Even if it's a simple five-, twenty-, or sixty-minute ride from Point A to Point B, in that moment, you can share the most intimate or most frivolous human connection with another.

Now turn the page and hop into the passenger's seat as I take you for a ride through my experiences behind the wheel.

Jonathan K Wong

Jonathan Wong
Honolulu, Hawaii

CHAPTER 1
FREAKS COME OUT AT NIGHT

Driving for Uber and Lyft is probably one of the most fun side gigs you'll ever take on, especially if you're a people person. It's convenient—you get to set your own hours because you simply log on to the app, make yourself available to accept rides, and BOOM—off you go!

The most interesting passengers, though, come out at night. It's after work, so people are stressed and ready to relax, release, and have some fun!

In this first chapter, I'll be sharing with you some of my funniest and most interesting stories from driving around Honolulu, Hawaii. As we all know, "freaks come out at night."

TALES FROM BEHIND THE WHEEL

"Have You Accepted Jesus Christ as Your Lord and Savior?"

I had a typical pickup call from a Waikiki hotel, so off I went once the app pinged. When I rolled up to the hotel, these two guys got into my car with their smartphones blaring some gangsta rap songs. I chuckled to myself since the guys getting into my car were as white as rice, but here they were pounding out some tunes like they were a couple of O.G.s (original gangsters).

"Where to?" I asked since they hadn't entered their destination.

"Oh, we're not sure yet. Just head down toward the zoo, and we'll figure it out and let you know," said one man with a distinctly effeminate lisp. Yup, I had picked up a gay couple! It was clear these guys were pretty zonked already since they were having a good old time playing with each other in the back, making jokes and remarks, and all the while, dancing out to their gangsta tunes.

I have nothing against gay people, but the image of two white, gay males, rocking out to gangsta rap in the backseat of an Uber was a hilarious sight!

FREAKS COME OUT AT NIGHT

This is...bizarre, I thought to myself while driving down Kalakaua Avenue.

When we got near the zoo, the man told me, "You can pull in here for now." So I pulled into the zoo parking lot. "We're gonna get off here," he said. *Okay*, I thought to myself. We had barely gone a half mile and the ride hadn't lasted five minutes.

After they piled out of the car, one of them turned to me and asked, "Have you accepted Jesus Christ as your Lord and Savior yet?"

"Jesus and I are good," I replied.

"We're Jehovah's Witnesses, and we want to leave you with this gift," he replied.

Then they presented me with a fairly beat-up Bible, closed the door, and headed off, dancing to gangsta rap and starting to make out again with each other.

I looked down at the Bible and thought to myself, *They probably stole it from the hotel.*

As I drove off looking for my next ride, I couldn't help laughing and thinking, *Gay gangsta rap-loving, Jehovah's Witnesses—I*

TALES FROM BEHIND THE WHEEL

never thought there'd be such a thing. Looking back, I'm kind of wondering whether I got trolled on some obscure YouTube, Periscope, or Snapchat channel for my reaction. Gotta love the inter-webs!

Epilogue:

The next day, my girlfriend took the car to work while I stayed home. Later, when I looked on her Facebook and Instagram pages, I saw she had tagged me in a post with an image of the Bible I had left on my passenger's seat and the comment, "What were you doing last night?"

"We Need to Get Some Pussy"

Weekend evenings are the domain of the drunks—bar none. One of the rides that sticks out for me is a hotel pickup I had in Waikiki; I believe it was the Beach Marriott. When I pulled in, four military-looking guys piled in—and they were *plastered*. And it was only 3 p.m. Weekend hotel party off base?

When I say "plastered," I mean, they were *plastered.* They were already wasted, laughing, and joking, and ready to hit the

FREAKS COME OUT AT NIGHT

clubs. Their conversation was hilarious. As they piled into the car, they were talking about the pornos they had been watching in their room and all the pussy they wanted to nail that night.

"Where to?" I asked since they hadn't entered their destination in the rideshare app.

"We just need to get to Lewers Street. You can take a right over here," said the lead guy, referring to Kalakaua Avenue.

"Sorry," I said. "That's a one-way street. I can't turn there."

"My bad," he replied.

"Anywhere specific on Lewers?" I asked.

The lead guy asked his friends, "Hey, where are we heading, boys? Kelly's? Moose's?"

"I don't know; what about RumFire?" one guy asked.

"No, that's somewhere else, man," replied the third.

"Yeah, just Lewers; we'll decide when we get there," the first guy instructed me.

So off I went back down Kuhio heading toward Lewers.

TALES FROM BEHIND THE WHEEL

For the next five to ten minutes or so, I had four very drunk, very horny guys bouncing up and down, laughing in my car, rating all the hookers we were passing by. I must have heard the word "pussy" at least a hundred times.

When I got to Lewers and turned onto it, the lead guy said, "You can stop here, by the ABC Store. We need to get some cash from the ATM." I pulled over and let them out. Off they went to withdraw some money, still planning on getting lots of pussy.

"Good God!" I muttered to myself as I rolled out, the smell of alcohol still lingering in the air.

"Can We Stop at the Convenience Store?"

One evening, I received a ride request from the Punahou area, and off I went to pick up my fare like on any other night. When I pulled up to the pickup location, out comes this college-age kid. When he got into my car, he seemed friendly enough. We made small talk like I do with most passengers, but while he was very friendly, it became very clear that he was also quite stoned!

FREAKS COME OUT AT NIGHT

Several minutes into the ride, he asked me, "Can we stop at the convenience store around the corner?"

"Sure," I said and pulled over.

"I'll be right back," he said.

He went in while I waited. After a few minutes, my thoughts got the better of me and I said to myself, *I hope he's not robbing the place and I'm his getaway ride....*

Fortunately, he had simply gone in to get a drink and snack and then we were off again. Ever the friendly kid, he offered me some of his chips, but I politely declined. Then I dropped him off at home and called it a night.

College Girls

The University of Hawaii (UH) dorms are a very common pick-up and drop-off point on weekend evenings. Here, the battle of the sexes is very clear. Carloads of girls vs. carloads of guys, and they each have their own party styles, as if trying to outdo the other sex. I find college girls infinitely more fun to pick up; they're wilder in the fun sense, and they make funnier and more intelligent jokes. Plus, it doesn't hurt that they're incredibly gorgeous.

Much more social, college girls will often take pictures, Snapchat, or Vine our rides. When asked, I'll play along and say, "Hi" to their feeds.

Once in a while, they'll ask me, "Do you go to UH too?" or "What are you majoring in?" Infinitely flattered by their attention, I often reply, "Thanks, but I'm old enough to be your dad," as I drop them off with surprised looks on their faces. And no, I don't get their numbers, but I know other guys who do.

Uber Is the New Tinder

It's not only college girls, but lots of working women heading out for a night on the town who use Uber or Lyft to get safely to the bar or club. One night, after dropping off a bunch of UH girls in Waikiki, I picked up a group of women near Ala Moana heading to M Nightclub. It's interesting to see the contrast ten years can make. These women were more mature in their conversation, but they were still out and having just as much fun.

FREAKS COME OUT AT NIGHT

As we made small talk, I shared with them that I'd just dropped off a carload of UH girls looking for a fun time. "We're just like them, but just ten years older," one woman told me. Their conversations revolved around work dramas as opposed to homework or exams. Like their younger counterparts, though, they were still very much interested in meeting cute guys for fun.

"So, have you ever gone home with any of the girls you pick up?" one of the girls asked.

"No, I have a girlfriend already, so I'm not here for that," I replied.

"Oh, that's too bad," she said. "We meet cute Uber drivers all the time. Haven't you heard? Uber's the new Tinder."

"Oh, you don't say?" I replied. "We'll, I'm happily spoken for, but I'm always happy to give you guys this type of ride."

We all shared a laugh. Then I dropped them off at M, wished them a fun night, and headed off to my next ride.

And yes, I have heard of and even know single guys looking for action who drive for Uber or Lyft to hook up. Guys, if you're among them, just don't be creeps.

TALES FROM BEHIND THE WHEEL

"Shaka, Shaka!"

One night, I picked up a couple from a restaurant in Waikiki. When we started chatting, she told me she was recently divorced and had just moved to Hawaii from somewhere on the Mainland. He had lived here for a few years, and they had been friends for a long time. She was here to relax and figure out what she wanted to do next in her life.

We drove down the road, heading back toward their apartment, singing along to the car radio and joking all the way. Then he asked me about "Shaka Shaka-ing." It was clear from his question that "Shaka, Shaka" was apparently some Mainland transplant code word. As the couple joked about "Shaka, Shaka-ing," I realized this divorcée might not necessarily be with the love of her life, but it sounded like her needs were being met. That was nice to know—everybody deserves some good loving. Shaka, Shaka!

"We Can All Take Turns with Her"

One night, I picked up a bunch of folks at a Kailua bar, and oh,

FREAKS COME OUT AT NIGHT

boy! It was a larger group than I could accommodate, so they haggled with me about fitting everyone in. "She can sit on my lap," said one guy. I stood my ground, though, because as the driver, I want everyone to be safe and in a seatbelt. (That and it's the law!)

Finally, they agreed to request a second car, so I took the first group off. "So and so's house, right?" someone in the second group said to one of my passengers as I was heading out. "Yeah, we'll see you there," the sober one in my car replied.

One sober guy. The rest of my passengers were composed of one *really* drunk guy, who was the haggler; a drunk or stoned college-age-looking girl, and one quiet person who never really said anything.

It was a twenty-minute ride from Kailua to the house they were heading to. It certainly sounded like the night was *not* over for these guys.

"They have more beers waiting and pizza," said Sober Guy.

"She's always good," Haggler replied.

"Yeah, she is; we did it last weekend," Sober Guy said.

TALES FROM BEHIND THE WHEEL

A minute or so later, Haggler shared, "Just got a text from her. She can't wait to see you."

He continued, "You know, she likes it when you...." I decided to tune out at that point, but a few minutes later, I heard, "We can try her together; you know she likes that."

Conversation continued on this subject and others with Drunk Girl chiming in on random stuff. Then she took out her cigarette lighter and started to light it in my car. Thankfully, Sober Guy corrected her before I needed to and she put the lighter away.

Toward the end of the ride, Haggler said, "Hey, you're a real fun driver. Let me get your card. We'd love to have you pick us up regularly on our nights out."

"Sorry, I'm out of cards," I lied.

When we got to the house, I dropped them off.

Before leaving, Haggler said to me, "Hey, if you need a break, feel free to come in."

"I'm good, bro. Thanks," I replied. "Have a good evening."

Then I headed off.

FREAKS COME OUT AT NIGHT

From the sound of what they had planned, I'm sure they had a good evening. But I was good, too.

Costume Party

It was toward the end of a Friday night for me. I'd been driving several hours when a request came in for a pickup several miles away, deep in one of the valleys surrounding Honolulu. Rides like those are nice on the one hand because they tend to be longer, so you have more time to chat with the riders. On the other hand, they kind of suck because it does take a while to get to them, but I'm always glad for the work.

So I headed off to the pickup location, which was a house up on a hill off of a side street in a beautiful neighborhood. When I arrived at the house, out came a couple wearing costumes—a Caucasian gentleman in sixteenth-century European garb and an Asian woman dressed as a Geisha. I did a double-take since it was the middle of summer—not Halloween—but it was quite obvious they were leaving a costume party.

Once they got into my car, off we went, and they started chatting with me. They were a married couple who had met back in grad school. They confirmed they had just come from a friend's costume party. We had a fun time chuckling about their outfits and the costumes the other party-goers had been wearing. Professionally, it turns out we all had a lot in common since both were university instructors and researchers. Nerds know how to have fun too.

Going Home with the Stripper

One night, I got a request from one of the districts in our area that has lots of hostess bars and strip clubs. The exact business location wasn't named on the request, but I was pretty sure it was one of the clubs. When I arrived, out came a couple—an obviously half-naked woman covered by a jacket and a male companion. As they got into my car, I struggled *not* to stare at the half-naked woman sitting behind me since it was just a little awkward for me.

As I drove them home, we made small talk. Then the woman declared how hungry she was. Her companion reassured her he'd either make something after they got in or he'd order

FREAKS COME OUT AT NIGHT

something out. From the conversation, it was obvious the male companion was a good friend and not a random hookup. Still though, he was lucky to "go home with the stripper" for whatever it was worth.

The Stripper's Early Night

Several months later, I got another pickup request from the same bar. When I arrived, out came another woman who was obviously a stripper. She was all by herself. Oddly enough, it was still early into the night.

She got in and we were off. She began venting about the long night and how disrespectful a lot of the male customers were. It got to the point where she just needed some room to breathe, so her boss had given her the rest of the night off.

We went for an extended ride since she said she was hungry, so I took her through a restaurant drive-thru. We talked at length about her job, her goals, her desire to transition into a career in healthcare once she finished school, and other jobs she wanted to take in the meantime once she ended her dancing days.

TALES FROM BEHIND THE WHEEL

When we reached her home after a fairly long ride, she got out with a smile on her face. I was glad for that since when she entered my car, her face reflected frustration. She thanked me for the ride and for letting her eat her meal while we drove. She waved as I drove off. Through the rearview mirror, I watched her disappear into her home, a little worn for wear, but much better than she had looked when we first met.

Sometimes, one of the cool things about being a rideshare driver is just being the friendly ear to whom a person who had a long rough day at work can vent. And it doesn't hurt when the person venting is an attractive young woman.

The Ride of Shame

One of the most chuckle-worthy experiences as a rideshare driver happens on Saturday and Sunday mornings when you get calls from riders to pick them up at someone's home.

One Sunday morning, I got a pickup request from a man in a residential neighborhood. When I arrived, out came a woman in a nice dress. As she got into my car, I confirmed the request-

FREAKS COME OUT AT NIGHT

er's name since it was obvious her name could not be "Shane." She confirmed that the ride was hers, but "He was nice enough to pay for it." Despite her remark, she was shaking her head as if frustrated.

When I inquired how she was doing that morning, she said she'd had a long night, needed to get home, and was ready for a shower. I also noticed her dress and makeup looked a bit worn.

After I dropped her off at her home, she went inside, looking a little worn-out.

On another occasion, on a Wednesday morning, I got a pickup request from another residential neighborhood. I assumed I would be taking someone to work for a mid-morning shift. Out came a guy looking a little worse for wear asking me to take him to a shopping center a few miles off where he had left his car.

As we rode, I asked him how his night had gone. He said it had been fun and filled with a lot of drinking with his friends and a group of young women they'd met. I said how awesome and fun that sounded, but then he shook his head and said he should have gone straight home instead because the evening hadn't been so great for him since he and his new lady friend had never really clicked. I expressed my regret for the not-as-fun end to his evening.

After I dropped him off to retrieve his car and rolled away, I was glad I was not the one with regrets and taking the notorious ride of shame.

"Get Her Home Safe, or Else!"

It was a Friday night, around 11 p.m., when I got a ride request from a Chinatown bar. As I pulled up to the bar, a whole group of women approached my car. "This should be fun," I told myself.

Only one girl got into my car. Meanwhile all of her girlfriends were asking me to make sure she got home safely. Girlfriend 1 took a picture of me and my car. Girlfriends 2, 3, and 4 made me promise to get her home safely, one adding in an "or else" as she waved her camera phone at me.

I headed out with the girls' precious cargo. My passenger was slightly buzzed, but we had a nice conversation about her grad-

FREAKS COME OUT AT NIGHT

uate studies, her career, and how she and her friends had been out for a night on the town to celebrate a friend's candidacy for public office. It turned out we had a great deal in common since we had studied for the same undergraduate and graduate degrees. She apologized to me for her friends, saying they were just a little overprotective. I brushed it off, understanding their concern due to high profile events that had recently happened and been all over the news. (An Uber driver had been arrested and accused of raping a female passenger not two weeks prior).

I dropped her off at her home, keeping my promise to her friends and knowing that the "Or else!" wasn't really directed at me.

"Drive-Thru, Please"

One common request I get from late night clubbers and bar hoppers, especially in groups or couples, is the "Drive-thru, please" request. Folks always want their munchies and will ask me to take them to Jack in the Box, Taco Bell, or McDonald's. I always oblige, not wanting to deny a starving human.

TALES FROM BEHIND THE WHEEL

Many drivers will often deny requests, saying, "I'm not paid to wait," or they will ask for a generous tip in return for fulfilling it. In my way of thinking, the customer is always right (most of the time), and I know how sucky it is to be hungry.

I may not be "paid to wait," but I know the value of working with a customer to provide good service, and my faith is almost always rewarded with a free taco or two, a free sandwich, or even a full meal. Score!

CHAPTER 2
HERE ON BUSINESS

Bed on a Boat

Business travelers are always a core group of rideshare passengers needing rides to and from meetings and accommodations. One of my first eye-opening experiences was picking up a business traveler in Waikiki from a restaurant. When I arrived, he was slightly buzzed and smelled of alcohol. He requested that I take him to the marina. I thought that a strange drop-off point, but I obliged.

Off we went, and we had a nice chat on the way. It turned out that he was a traveling consultant and trainer working with organizations to prepare people for the Project Management Institute's PMP exam. I perked up at this because I had studied Project

TALES FROM BEHIND THE WHEEL

Management in graduate school, and being an experienced project manager, I had always wanted to sit for the PMP. When I asked what company he worked for, he shared that he was self-employed. We talked at length about the PMP exam and the PMI, and then he offered me his card to share with anyone wanting to sit for the exam, adding "I'll throw you a bone."

When I asked why he wanted to go to the marina, he said that whenever he travels, being self-employed, he just needed the most basic of accommodations—a place to sleep. He'd found a great deal on Airbnb for a bed on a boat in the marina for just $20 a night.

I have to laugh at just how many people rent on Airbnb, the types of accommodations people provide, and how many people jump at what. Being an Airbnb user myself, I have found great deals for accommodations, but I never thought "a bed on a boat" would be one of them.

I dropped off my self-employed, deep-discount traveler, wished him well, and drove off to my next request, still marveling at sleeping on a bed on a boat.

HERE ON BUSINESS

Airbnb *Everywhere*

From driving around associated tourists and business travelers, I've become truly amazed by just how many people are in the Airbnb business and what types of dwellings and units are rented. I've picked up Airbnb travelers at single family homes, *lots* of condominium complexes, and even public housing units in addition to the aforementioned "bed on a boat."

The "sharing economy" is truly a magnificent thing. Prior to selling my home a few years back, I, too, had contemplated getting into the Airbnb business since I had excess capacity to spare and definitely would have loved the extra income. I knew I would have made bank had I pursued it. I did not, however, for a couple of reasons: 1) Honolulu's bed and breakfast and transient accommodation laws, and 2) my homeowner's association regulations for my community. The last thing I needed was the tax collectors coming after me for operating an illegal bed and breakfast!

Of course, this situation is common across the country as local and state governments grapple with who regulates sharing economy services like Uber, Lyft, and Airbnb, and they pass laws outlining tax collection, insurance, and licensing regulations.

TALES FROM BEHIND THE WHEEL

In the meantime, I drive around marveling that I may be one of the only folks not doing Airbnb. (Curse you, you urge to be a law-abiding citizen!) I often think what my life would be like had I not sold my home a few years back and rented out my three extra bedrooms.

I then weep on the way back to my little apartment, driving my little sedan, as opposed to laughing all the way to the bank in my nonexistent BMW or Audi.

Nordstrom Grand Opening

Quite often, I pick up business travelers in town for retail companies that are opening new stores in Hawaii. Such was the case with Nordstrom, which relocated a store to a new Hawaii location. For several days, I picked up numerous Nordstrom employees and retail partners for various brand names who were in town to open the store. Every single one was a beautiful professional woman in either a business suit or tourist wear if on downtime. Whether I was shuttling them to and from Nordstrom to their hotels, or to Honolulu's hiking trails or beaches, I was amazed by just how big Nordstrom is given the volume of Nordstrom-related rides I had.

HERE ON BUSINESS

Well, I suppose it's not that surprising given that Nordstrom is a big and prestigious retailer. Of course, I'm not too familiar with its product lines since they're a bit out of my budget as a humble Uber and Lyft driver.

The International Marketplace

Complementing Nordstrom's reopening, Honolulu also recently renovated and relaunched the famous International Marketplace in Waikiki. As a driver daily shuttling tourists to and through the Waikiki beachfront district, I constantly passed by the marketplace and literally saw it rise from the ground up.

Over this time period, I picked up various construction contractors and managers connected to the project, including an experienced consultant who hoped his work on the project would translate into a huge promotion, and a California-based project manager/contractor who had ties to Hawai'i and looked and spoke like a local. (He had only lived in Hawaii briefly and was raised in California.)

There was such a sharp contrast between the refined and elegant women who were here to open Nordstrom and the rough and rugged construction contractors here to work on the International Marketplace. Gender differences are definitely real!

The Conference-Goer

As you might expect, one of the most common business travelers is the conference-goer. As with many major cities, Honolulu is a very popular conference destination with venues such as the Hawaii Convention Center, various Waikiki hotels, and the University of Hawaii all playing hosts to various conventions.

In particular, I always have a soft spot for academics who are in town for conferences. They make me hearken me back to a previous lifetime before I became an entrepreneur, moonlighting in the gig and freelance economy and promoting my own ventures.

One particular day, I made several runs to the University of Hawaii, which was hosting an agricultural conference. I had run several trips between faculty housing to the campus and from Waikiki to the campus, dropping off attendees. One Waikiki pickup was a husband and wife whom I had assumed were just like any other tourists about to go sightseeing. It turned out she was confer-

HERE ON BUSINESS

ence bound and needed to get ready for her presentation. He was sightseeing bound. They both agreed he got the better end of the deal. I've been there, done that as someone who's had a significant other tag along on trips. While I had to attend conference sessions, she would go sightseeing or shopping without me!

RIMPAC

The military market is *huge* in Hawaii and other parts of the nation for rideshare drivers, given the number of our courageous servicemen and women who do not have their own cars. Every few years, Hawaii plays host to an international war games between various navies of the Asia and Pacific rim nations called RIMPAC (the Rim of the Pacific Exercise). When RIMPAC hits, rideshare profits go through the roof because numerous ships from various countries sail into Honolulu with thousands of sailors, and they are all looking for recreation in Honolulu—and the rides that facilitate that.

During RIMPAC, I enjoyed one of my most profitable and enjoyable times as a driver. I gave nonstop rides all day long between the naval base, the Waikiki beachfront, and the downtown—an easy $20 fare each way, and during Surge (busy) times drivers get paid exponentially more—even double or triple. I enjoyed meeting our service members and their families and also service members from several different nations. That is one of the true joys of the job—meeting people from all over the world, learning their stories, and sharing with them Hawaii's culture and history. And, of course, getting our brave but drunk sailors, soldiers, airmen, and Marines back to base in one piece.

"I'm the Western Regional Representative for ____."

Another common business person I've picked up overtime is the "Western Regional Representative for [insert name of company here]." These folks in particular are always fascinating to pick up and chat with to learn about the work they do for their respective companies and what it's like to live out of a suitcase since most of them are on the road four days a week as they make the circuit, servicing their regions and clients.

I've picked up medical equipment suppliers servicing our area hospitals, software company reps servicing clients in town, a military contractor, and a trainer for Coca-Cola. Traveling across the country visiting accounts in different states sounds fun because

HERE ON BUSINESS

you get to travel all the time. However, it also sounds quite tiring since a lot of these people mention their inability to have much of a social life. My favorite comment from one of these folks is: "It's not cool having to pay high rent for a place you're only sleeping in two nights a week." I would imagine that would suck! Maybe they could just rent a storage unit for all their stuff and Airbnb it.

"I Flew Eight Hours for a Half-Hour Meeting."

Probably my favorite business travel tale from Year One comes from an attorney I picked up in downtown Honolulu who was heading back to Waikiki after a meeting. He had literally flown in during the middle of the night from the East Coast and was flying out again later that evening. He was heading back to his hotel for some quick R&R and sightseeing before needing to head back to the airport for his flight home. He'd left the night before on short notice from D.C. to make it to an early morning meeting with a client in downtown Honolulu whose case had suddenly come up. He literally stated, "I flew eight hours for a half-hour meeting." In all, the dude would have flown about sixteen hours (not counting layover times) for a half-hour meeting, and then had maybe five hours of sightseeing and downtime. That's a lot of time away from home and family for not that much work. Must be nice to make the big bucks....

Beauties and the Beast

I once had the privilege to pick up a group of models hired for Monster Energy for a promotional event Monster was doing in conjunction with the monthly Eat the Street event at the Makers and Tasters' food truck park and marketplace. Most of the models were local, but as part of the event, I also got to chauffeur around some of the Monster execs from out of town. I didn't get a picture with the models, but I did make a cameo appearance in their IG and Snapchat feeds that evening. They never gave me their names or IG IDs to follow, so I never did see the pictures. Oh well. It was nice just to know that even for a brief fifteen minutes, this beast got to be with a carload of beauties.

CHAPTER 3
CELEBRITY SIGHTINGS

Brushes with Greatness

One of the cool things about being a rideshare driver is you truly never do know who will get into your car, and occasionally, someone who is *somebody* gets in. I haven't personally given any real "A" listers a ride, but some of my friends have been very fortunate to drive some major celebrities. Daniel Dae Kim of *Lost* and *Hawaii Five-0* fame is someone who commonly makes the rounds on Uber and Lyft. I've had a bunch of friends pick him up; sometimes, he's in the company of Jorge Garcia, also of *Lost* and *Hawaii Five-0* fame. In this chapter, I'll share some tales of myself and some of my friends brushing elbows with greatness.

TALES FROM BEHIND THE WHEEL

The Local DJ

The first celebrity I ever picked up was one of local flavor. When I got the pickup request, I recognized the name immediately. Since the pickup location was the address and location of one of our local radio offices, it pretty much confirmed whom I thought it was. Once I pulled up in front of the office, into my car climbed one of our well-known local DJs and TV personalities.

"You are the first celebrity I've ever picked up doing this!" I exclaimed.

Chuckling, he replied, "I don't know about being a 'celebrity,' but thank you."

Since I was a former DJ (at an obscure independent station most people probably never heard of), we talked a bit about the radio industry. Our conversation shifted briefly to a huge local event (Diner En Blanc) he had been organizing for the past few years that I was looking forward to attending again.

As our ride wound down, I was fascinated when he shared that he didn't own a car and pretty much traveled by Uber daily to and from work and to other appointments. He was not the first nor last

CELEBRITY SIGHTINGS

person who's shared that fact with me, but it still fascinates me how much rideshare has changed the way we commute around town. For many people, the affordable pricing of rideshare has done away with the need to own and operate an automobile. Looking at my personal budget and expenses over the years, I know *very* well how much I spend operating a car between maintenance (always a killer), fuel costs, parking fees, insurance, and financing (when I couldn't pay outright). I know I'd save a ton not owning a car, and I often think to myself how much I could save riding the bus (too inconvenient), or in this day and age, ridesharing everywhere. I'm willing to bet my annual Uber or Lyft bill would be cheaper than what I pay in auto costs.

Comic-Con!

In the past few years, Honolulu has become quite the hotbed of comic-cons with Honolulu now hosting three each year. We're not quite San Diego, but our geek culture level is over 9,000—that's a *Dragon Ball Z* anime series reference for you non-geeks.

With three comic-cons each year, some major names started to be attracted to Hawaii, so our friendly neighborhood Uber and

TALES FROM BEHIND THE WHEEL

Lyft drivers were bound to start picking up some celebrities. I'll share the stories of two driver friends who were so fortunate.

A fellow driver had the fortune to pick up comic book legend Jim Lee of X-Men, WildCATS, Superman, and Batman fame. It's awesome to know that even a world famous artist uses the convenience of Uber and Lyft when traveling the globe to promote the awesomeness of comic books as opposed to renting and driving a car himself.

Another driver friend had the privilege of picking up famous cosplayer Jessica Nigri. He even had time to pose for photos with her, which made their way on to social media. Lucky guy! It's quite the day and age when people can leverage their hobby of dressing up as their favorite comic, anime, or video game characters into an actual career! If only I were that photogenic! I guess it helps if you're a hot female instead of a middle-aged guy.

Awards Night

The Na Hoku Hanohano Awards is the annual awards show for

CELEBRITY SIGHTINGS

the local music industry here in Hawaii. It's our version of the Grammys. On Hoku award night, several hours after the show ended, I received a very random ride request to pick up a group of guys. I rolled up and the guys piled in. At first, I thought it was just another group of guys finishing their night of partying, but once we got to talking, it turned out they were members of a band and had been post-partying after the Hokus. I actually recognized the name of the band, but being a band, I had no idea what the individual guys looked like, so I wouldn't have recognized them from Adam. Still, it was darn cool that I got to pick up an award-nominated band on awards night of all nights.

Since the energy was still contagious from the awards show and after-party in Waikiki, we were singing and having a good time all the way back to one of the member's homes, where I dropped everyone off. I'm glad I was able to get the band members home safe and sound, given the alcohol levels running through their veins. My rideshare colleagues and I provide this same safety service each and every day for people from all walks of life. Our work *does* make a big difference in saving lives.

TALES FROM BEHIND THE WHEEL

The Big Business Executive

It was a weekday morning, bright and early. I decided to drive the morning shift to catch all the commuters. I got a request for a pickup at one of the more upscale condos and headed there. When I pulled in, I picked up a gentleman not unlike a lot of other gentlemen I'd picked up a hundred times before. He named his destination as one of the high-rise office buildings in town, and then off we went. We chatted for a bit, talking about where we both grew up and the work he did. It turned out we had quite a bit in common. We grew up in the same town. We went to the same elementary school. He worked in publishing as an editor. I had studied some journalism in college. (My major was communication, but I did take some journalism classes.)

Then he mentioned the name of the publication he worked for. I was impressed because it was the largest business newspaper in town, which I'd followed for *years*. I complimented him and his colleagues on an outstanding publication, which he was happy to hear. Like many passengers before him, he shared that he "Ubers" several times a week to work because it's more convenient than driving. I pulled up to his office build-

CELEBRITY SIGHTINGS

ing and wished him a great day. We exchanged cards. When I looked down to read his card, I saw he was more than just "an editor." He was *the* editor.

Color me amazed at driving a down-to-earth, humble big honcho who runs a major paper to the office.

Five Minutes of Fame on Snapchat and Periscope

One of the amazing things about this day and age of smartphones and live streams is the simple fact that everyone can be a "minor celebrity." We all have our followers, be they a few hundred to a few thousand. (I have about 2,000–5,000 on each of my social media streams.) One of my favorite guilty pleasures is whenever someone gets in my car while broadcasting, whether it be on Periscope, Snapchat, Vine, or Facebook Live. I've driven passengers who are just sharing their day with their viewers. I've driven carloads of girls Snapchatting. I always get a kick out of it when I get the obligatory "Shout out to our Uber driver; what's your name again? Jon! This is our Uber driver, Jon!"

TALES FROM BEHIND THE WHEEL

I have no idea how big these passengers' channels and followings are, but it's pretty funny to think how I'm on a pseudo-reality show/social media stream while rolling down the street to take these people from point A to point B, and it's being viewed by all of their followers. Hopefully, they're filming my good side.

CHAPTER 4
THE EVERYDAY RIDER

We Keep the Town Moving

Most people who think of rideshare driving assume it's mostly tourists and drunks who take Ubers and Lyfts. While tourists and drunks/partiers do constitute a good portion of the business, everyday people who need to get to work, school, home, or to appointments constitute an equally big share of the business. I do take a certain pride in knowing the work my rideshare colleagues and I do ultimately helps keep our town moving. If it weren't for us, people wouldn't be able to get to and from work or school, to home, to their doctor appointments, or to fetch their groceries.

TALES FROM BEHIND THE WHEEL

Gone Grocery Shopping

When I first started driving, I was actually amazed by how many ride requests I'd get to and from places such as Safeway, Don Quijote, Walmart, and Sam's Club, and just how many types of people would be loading up my car with their groceries.

Often, it was college-age kids without cars who were doing their grocery runs. Late nights seem to be a popular grocery time for college kids. Makes sense, I guess, since they are studying all day. I always chuckled at how spoiled they were since I distinctly remember when I was a college student either needing to catch the bus with my groceries, *walk*, or wait until I could borrow my parents' car. As a college kid back in the late '90s, I could only dream about tapping a button on my phone and having a dude in a car magically appear within a few minutes to whisk me and my groceries home.

Older adults without a car (mostly women) are also a popular group that relies on Uber and Lyft for grocery runs. They usually prefer to do their shopping during the day. Being older and with more money, they also tend to tip generously, especially if you help to unload the groceries to their door.

THE EVERYDAY RIDER

The grocery-errand market is a pretty nice market to build a clientele around since some people, particularly older adults, enjoy working with a regular driver they can depend on.

The Doctor's Appointment

Over the year, I lost count of how many people I've taken or picked up from doctor's appointments and even actual hospitalizations in need of a ride home. Routine doctor's visits. Urgent Care. Dialysis treatments. Just released from the hospital. You name it, I've dropped them off or picked them up. Medical transport is very much a legitimate market that a driver can build a decent clientele and business around. It works for ambulances! Of course, as a rideshare driver, you definitely do not want a person on the verge of death riding in your car, but a routine doctor's appointment is all good!

Probably my best medical story from Year One revolves around a woman I picked up who wanted a ride to the ER because of her swollen foot. And boy, was it swollen! She couldn't sit in the passenger's seat like normal but needed to tilt and rest her foot on the seat. Ironically, she lived in the same apartment building

TALES FROM BEHIND THE WHEEL

I had lived in during my grad school years, so seeing that old address and pulling into that old driveway brought back memories. Seeing the poor woman hobble and hop into my car was something else.

The hospital wasn't too far, so the ride itself was all of not even ten minutes and probably not far north of $6 or $7. Beats paying a few hundred on her end for a 911 call for an ambulance, I guess. Of course, I doubt her health insurance covers "Emergency Uber Rides."

Daily Commute

It's a story I heard oft-repeated over the course of the year from people I would drive daily going to work: "Oh, yeah, I love Uber/Lyft. I take it to work every day. Beats owning/maintaining/driving a car or taking the bus!"

I continue to be amazed by how much ridesharing has changed the way many of us commute daily. And like my business executive and local media personalities whom I talked about in Chapter 3, I have driven daily rideshare commuters of all walks

THE EVERYDAY RIDER

of life to and from work: downtown business people, retail workers at the mall or Waikiki beachfront, restaurant workers, bartenders, security guards, college professors, medical doctors, nurses, etc. All have ridden with me to work and from work and shared that this is their daily routine. They all say it's cheaper than operating their own car.

Knowing the pay disparity between a retail associate at The Gap, a server at California Pizza Kitchen, or a guard at Securitas vs. the pay of a tenured university professor or a nurse or physician at a major hospital, I am quite shocked that people at very different socio-economic levels of society all find paying your friendly neighborhood Uber driver around $15 or $20 per day works out better than operating a car every day. But then, when I add up what I pay each year in car payments, insurance, maintenance, gas, and parking and do the math myself, it does seem paying $400 a month for Uber works out to be cheaper than car payments, gas, auto insurance, parking fees, or car maintenance. It's not as cheap as taking the bus or metro, but it's way more convenient.

TALES FROM BEHIND THE WHEEL

Swing Shift

As a rideshare driver, you get a good feel for how work shifts are organized in the different industries and sectors of your town's economy. Prior to moonlighting as a rideshare driver and transitioning into a writing career, I spent my entire adult life working in academia in a nice, stable government-funded job doing the traditional nine-to-five thing. Like most people, I'd be up around 6:00 a.m. and on the road shortly after to get to my office between 7:30 and 8:00 a.m. Then I'd be out of the office around 5:00 p.m. to fight traffic on the way home.

As a rideshare driver, you come to realize and appreciate that people are starting and ending work at all hours of the day and night, so you'll always get a ride request, no matter the time of day.

By driving during the day, I came to appreciate the work hours of retail associates, restaurant workers, and hotel workers who would be starting their work day anywhere between 10:00 a.m. and 2:00 p.m. for mid-day shifts. If I were out driving between 3:00 p.m. and 5:00 p.m., I could just as easily be picking up someone from home going to a job at a hotel, restaurant, or store for the swing shift as I could be picking up someone from the downtown business district, a bank, or military base who is calling it a day and ready to head home.

Having the freedom to set my own hours and pretty much drive whenever I felt like it, I took to the road whenever it suited me. In particular, I enjoyed driving graveyard hours.

The Graveyard Shift

Driving graveyard hours is such a guilty pleasure. Most people assume you drive all the alkies heading to and from the bar, but that's just half the story. Sure, you have people going out on weekday nights to the bar or club because they work swing shifts and don't need to be up early the next day—or maybe they do, but they have an alcohol problem; I'm not judging. I'm just glad when I can get them home safely.

Driving graveyards is actually an interesting mix because you get to see people's shift transitions. I've picked up retail workers, restaurant workers, grocery store workers, hotel workers, security guards, and even strippers who are getting off the swing shift. I've picked them up at 10:00 p.m., 11:00 p.m., 12:00 a.m., 1:00 a.m., 2:00 a.m., or 3:00 a.m. after they've finished cleaning the store and restaurant and balancing out their cash registers. As far as drop-offs go, I've dropped off security guards who work the graveyard shift at whatever properties they are watching overnight.

Who else do you see after 12:00 a.m. requesting an Uber or Lyft ride? Besides people going to or from work and the partier heading to or from the bar, another common occurrence is the midnight shopper! Yes, lots of folks do their shopping after midnight at the local twenty-four-hour Walmart or another grocery store or drugstore. I always chuckle when I get a request at 3:00 a.m. and the pickup reads Walmart, Don Quijote, Longs, or Walgreens.

And finally, yes, you guessed it. Deep nocturnal hours after midnight always produce people who need the ride of shame home. I'll pick up someone sporting a "freshly ****ed" hairdo, needing a ride home from his or her hook-up's place. Of course, sometimes it's not a ride of shame but rather someone clearly ripped who was just hanging out with friends, drinking and playing video games or cards or whatever. Those rides are infinitely less awkward than the rides of shame.

THE EVERYDAY RIDER

I Got Towed

Another pretty common and regular ride request I get is to take some poor soul to a local tow yard because he needs to get his car out of the lot after having had it towed away earlier in the day or the night before. More often than not, it's a morning ride because the person just woke up to realize his car was towed overnight for whatever reason. Not surprisingly, these folks are almost always irritated at the inconvenience. And things devolve more when they realize they need to pay somewhere around $200.00 in cash to get their car back.

The most memorable of these incidents involved an early morning pickup at a Waikiki hotel. My passenger was a soldier who'd attended a hotel party the night before. He had woken up to discover his car missing, and after making frantic phone calls, he learned his car had been towed overnight for some violation. He was extremely irritated, and all the way to the tow yard—a thirty-minute ride—he was fuming about the inconvenience and the highway robbery of needing to pay to get his car out of the lot. It definitely sucks to be towed…. I've been there myself!

CHAPTER 5
CAB WARS

Cab Drivers Gonna Hate

After driving for Uber and Lyft, I can empathize with and even feel bad for cab drivers. I remember the very first weekend I drove. I got a simultaneous drop-off and pickup at a popular Waikiki bar. As I rolled up, I passed a *long line* of cabs just waiting for a customer. I pulled up, dropped off a fare, and simultaneously picked up my new fare. I was in and out in all of thirty seconds. Meanwhile, all those cabs were just sitting there, idly waiting and basically begging for someone to ask for a ride. If looks could kill, I'd have been dead a hundred times over because about twenty cabbies were staring daggers at me.

Here are my thoughts on the cab industry and its drivers. I

feel for them. Ridesharing has forced a paradigm shift and is a truly disruptive technology (if you know change theory and diffusion of innovation theory). You have cabbies who are working in a *long*-entrenched industry with established laws, rules, and norms, and then, all of a sudden, you have this army of technology-enabled non-cabbies who perform very cab-like functions and are undercutting and taking away all of the cabbies' business. Most cabbies are business owners themselves, needing either to lease out their own cars and pay dispatch fees to their companies or to their respective transportation authorities, local governments, and what not. I know how much it would hurt me if all of a sudden I lost half my business to a bunch of upstarts. I'd be upset too.

Here, however, is where my compassion ends. If you've read my author bio, you'll know I have earned an MBA and also worked as a business consultant, so what comes up next is the MBA talking. In business, you always need to be responsive to changes in the industry and the external environment. When you see how the industry and society are changing, you need to evolve with the times. If you can't, you deserve to go out of business. That may sound harsh, but it is what it is. Darwinism applies in

CAB WARS

business just like everywhere else; it is most definitely survival of the fittest. In my humble opinion, cab drivers either need to improve their service and their business model, or, as they say, "If you can't beat 'em, join 'em." If I'd been a cab driver, I'd have smartened up and switched over to ridesharing a long time ago. It definitely beats watching guys with black U's or pink mustaches (Uber and Lyft's respective logos) on their cars zoom by me with riders while I wait on a curb, seething in anger and praying that somebody will want a ride. You need to adapt! Either provide a better service and value or get with the rideshare program!

Hassling with a Cab Driver

In my first few weeks of driving, I had a pickup request at a Waikiki Hotel. When I pulled into the hotel, my passenger was not there. However, a young female tourist walked up to my car to ask whether I could take her to the airport. I told her I couldn't since I already had a passenger I was waiting for. Since she didn't speak English very well, she didn't really understand me. Near us was a cab driver, who was hassling with her to get into his car. I suspect she'd called for a ride, but when the cab

TALES FROM BEHIND THE WHEEL

pulled up, she just didn't feel comfortable with the driver so she kept insisting that I take her while the cab driver was basically yelling at her to get in. Looking over at the cab driver, I told her that her ride was there (pointing at the cab). The driver was basically staring daggers into both of us, frustrated that I might steal a fare from him.

Eventually, I convinced the woman to go with the cab driver. He looked relieved when she finally did get in his vehicle. As he drove off, I waved at him and wished him a good evening. I'm sure he got the woman to the airport in one piece without assaulting her. It probably cost her an arm and a leg, but thankfully, I didn't get into a confrontation with an angry cab driver. Still, if I had an angry older man yelling at me to get into his car, I'd probably be reluctant to get into it too.... As for me, my sense of fair play paid off because my rider showed up just as the cab disappeared into the distance.

Rolling Up to the Bar

Driving late nights, half of your business is picking up folks at the bars and nightclubs. It's not uncommon to roll up to any given

CAB WARS

popular bar or nightclub and see a long line of cabs waiting for folks to come out and ask for a ride. It's tougher on cab drivers now since rideshare is basically a third of the cost of a cab.

It's perfectly normal for me to roll up on Lewers Street between 11 p.m. and 2 a.m. outside of Moose's or Kelley O'Neil's and see ten cabs waiting. It's an easy night if my passenger is outside waiting (like he's supposed to be) and he then gets in and we are off. It's an awkward night if my passenger is not ready (shame on you if this describes you!) and I need to wait while ten cabbies stare daggers at me.

The same scenario repeats at District or Republik at closing time. There's always a looooong line of cabs waiting outside. On those nights, I find it easier simply to wait across the street in the Ala Moana parking lot and just ninja in and out.

The Long Line at the Hilton

The Hilton Hawaiian Village is a popular pickup and drop-off location in Waikiki, and as with most popular spots, it always has a long lines of cabs waiting to be hailed. I did not realize just

TALES FROM BEHIND THE WHEEL

how long the line at the Hilton ran, though. On one occasion, I had a pickup at the Hilton, but because of construction traffic, I rerouted and wound up driving around the perimeter of the parking structure to get to the side street to go out the back way. I had *never* gone that way before (I didn't even know the route existed), but going through the perimeter of the parking structure, I was privy to seeing the looooooooooooooong line of cabs that literally wrapped around the entire parking structure. I was amazed. I know typical cab protocol calls for everyone to wait in line and take fares once it is your turn, and I'd seen cabs at the drop-off and pickup areas for years like everyone else. But never in my life had I imagined that the line stretched out of sight around the perimeter of the parking structure at least eighty cars long. If I had to follow cab protocol and wait in a line that stretched two to three blocks with eighty guys in front of me before I could give someone a ride, I'd be mad too when I saw a rideshare guy zooming in and out, bypassing the line, and picking up and dropping off riders oblivious to the "proper etiquette." It bites to be a cab driver.

CAB WARS

Tourist Spots

Cab driver lines also extend to popular tourist spots. The USS Arizona Memorial is a popular attraction where both cab drivers and rideshare drivers regularly get pickup and drop-off requests. On my first Arizona drop-off and pickup trips, I was oblivious to the rules and would pick up and drop off passengers in the parking lot like normal people.

Given that rideshare drivers are classified as "commercial drivers," though, facility rules dictate that we have to drop off and meet riders on the "commercial vehicle" side, which is basically where all the cab drivers will hang out. Unlike the cabs, though, we can zoom in and out since our passengers are already waiting, so it's not like we have to "wait in line" with the cabs for a passenger to hire us out.

So there I was, day in and day out, picking up and dropping folks off at the Arizona with lines of cab drivers eyeing me because I'm making bank and they're not. There are better occupations than being a cab driver in the Age of Rideshare.

TALES FROM BEHIND THE WHEEL

Parking Lot Break

As a rideshare driver, particularly if you're working a long shift or all day, you basically do assume the life of a cab driver, and you'll often need to wait for ride requests or take a break, which you do by sitting in a parking lot. It's pretty funny when cab drivers then pull up next to you to take their own breaks between fares. To make things less awkward, when I pull in for a stop, I will usually unmark my car, taking off my Uber and Lyft tags so I just blend in like any other shopper or diner who is just chilling in his car while waiting. In the past, sometimes I would pull into a lot and see a group of cabbies there chilling on their smoke break (the Ala Moana shopping center and the Safeway store on Pali are both infamous for this). When I'd roll up with my Uber and Lyft tags up, I could just see them starting to eye me, so I'd drive by and find somewhere else to park and rest.

Stink Eye on the Road

Since I have to share the road with others, it's not uncommon to see dozens of cabs driving around, hustling for fares. Waiting at stoplights or intersections, it is a *common* occurrence to

CAB WARS

look over and see a cab driver eyeing you. A fellow driver friend of mine once had a cabbie swing the wheel in his direction to sideswipe him. (Fortunately, I think this cab driver was an exception. Almost all cab drivers are law-abiding folks. They may be frustrated and angry, but they are not criminals).

It's sad that rideshare and cab drivers have to compete for fares. At the end of the day, we are all people just trying to provide for ourselves and our families. I can understand the anger and frustration on cab drivers' parts, but ultimately, they either need to improve their service and business model or make the transition to rideshare. Competition is a good thing because, ultimately, it benefits the consumer. So cab companies, I wish you the best and hope you can improve your services. To any cab drivers reading this, if you're interested in transitioning to becoming a rideshare driver, I welcome you to contact me. I'll be glad to help you get started.

CHAPTER 6

#GPSFAILS
WHEN GPS FAILS YOU

Let me first start by saying, "Thank God for GPS!" I cannot imagine doing this job if I had to rely on trying to read a map or on people's ability to give me directions. If it weren't for GPS, I would *not* have bothered taking on rideshare driving. Having said that, there's times when the GPS utterly, fantastically fails you and winds up dumping you nowhere near where you need to be. Presented in this chapter are some tales of such GPS failures.

The Long Way to the Airport

Airport rides are a good portion of the rideshare business. In a

TALES FROM BEHIND THE WHEEL

typical day, I might get four or five airport rides from the hotels in Waikiki, and typically, I get ecstatic because those are really good fares that help me reach my earnings' goal for the day in and of itself. What is strange, though, is the GPS route, which is a *long* roundabout route through the military base to the airport terminal that is: 1) very out of the way, and 2) probably not possible since the military will never allow you on base without the proper credentials. So I almost always turn off the GPS and follow the route to the airport that I've known by heart since I was a teenager when I would drive my mother to the airport for her quarterly Las Vegas vacation trips with her friends.

The route GPS recommends takes you through Joint Base Pearl Harbor Hickam, which is actually past the airport coming from Waikiki, and, according to the GPS, would take you an extra half hour. I have no clue why the GPS thinks that's a better route than taking the actual airport exit and saving twenty to thirty minutes of your time. Savvy passengers who look over at my GPS always ask me, "Wow, is it really going to take forty-five minutes to get there?" I always reply, "Oh, don't pay any attention to that, we'll be there in fifteen minutes! The GPS is crazy; I'll get you there in plenty of time for your flight." Sighs

#GPSFAILS

of relief then always emerge from my car passengers. The GPS has done this for a good year, and I have no idea whether it will ever correct itself, but it always elicits a raised eyebrow and a chuckle from me.

"I'm at the Back of the Hotel."

When I first started driving, a common pickup point would be the RumFire restaurant located at the Sheraton Waikiki. The GPS would always route me to the back of the hotel at the commercial loading dock. Not knowing exactly where RumFire was at the time or how to get to the Sheraton by itself, I would naively follow the GPS and then have to call my passengers and say, "I'm here; where are you?" They'd reply, "At the hotel pickup area." Then I'd have to say, "The GPS routed me to the back of the hotel; can you make it here?" They usually didn't know where that was, so I'd need to figure out how to get to the actual pickup area. Not knowing that RumFire was at the Sheraton, and most passengers not knowing which hotel they were at either, it was an exercise to figure out where to go since the GPS would always route me back to the rear of the hotel.

TALES FROM BEHIND THE WHEEL

In any event, eventually I figured out that the RumFire was in the Sheraton, and I learned the proper route to the hotel lobby drop-off so I could kindly ignore the GPS' crazy route to the loading dock. Eventually, the GPS corrected itself to the proper pickup point, but those initial months sucked whenever I would get a RumFire pickup request. To this day, I have no idea why GPS would ever think RumFire's patrons would walk to the hotel's back loading dock for a pickup. Perhaps the club itself is in the back of the hotel, so the loading dock is the nearest exit to the road? Ah, the joys of technology.

Back of the Complex

Similarly, I often get ride requests to pick up people at a various residential complexes. Many times, the GPS will take me to the opposite end of a complex from where my passenger is actually waiting. Upon arrival, there is no passenger, so I wind up calling or texting to see where the passenger is or if I'm even at the right place. Looking at the app on their phones, the passenger will see I'm at the opposite end of the complex, and then he'll either give me directions to his side of the complex, or he'll run

#GPSFAILS

to where I'm at, huffing and puffing to get in. Bottom line: GPS is not always accurate or reliable, but it's definitely much better to have a sometimes-wrong GPS than to be stuck trying to find my way around without it. If it weren't for GPS, my job would be nearly impossible or just outright suck.

Around the Block

Sometimes, passengers will not enter the actual address of their location, and as a result, the GPS will take you to an approximation of where they are located. Then you might wind up around the corner or even a block away from where the passenger actually is. On those occasions, it is not uncommon to arrive to no passenger, so you'll need to call to see where the person is, only to learn she is "around the corner," at which point, you drive to her or she'll walk to you. On one occasion, I had a pickup at a childcare facility in town, and the passenger, being an immigrant, barely spoke English. For whatever reason, she was *across the street*—waiting instead at the childcare facility. She had a difficult time communicating this to me, so I went around the block three times in a high traffic

TALES FROM BEHIND THE WHEEL

area, trying to find her and probably passing her several times without being waved down. I finally pulled over in front of the childcare facility (illegally) and stayed on the phone, telling her I was in front and what my car looked like, only to look across the street, and there she was with her kid. Luckily, no cops were around to give me a citation for an illegal pullover. Needless to say, I was quite irked by that point, but ultimately, she was a nice person, so I didn't totally kill her passenger rating. Since she didn't speak English, I gave her a break despite her poor communication skills.

"The Thing Says You're a Half-Mile Away."

Sometimes when GPS fails, it either completely hiccups or the user screws up majorly and drops his pin on the screen far from his pickup point. Upon arrival, the same old story happens; there is no passenger, so I wind up calling and saying, "Hey, it's Jon from Uber. I'm here outside your pickup point. Are you here?" The passenger will then look at his app and say, "It's weird. You're actually nowhere near where I am. You're like a half-mile/mile/few miles away. I'm at _____." At that point,

#GPSFAILS

I'm irked because I'll either still need to get to them, or I'll need to cancel the ride and eat the loss.

I have three worst examples of when this situation happened. The first occurrence happened relatively early in my driving career when I had a request in a neighborhood in one of the valleys to pick up a carload of college girls. The pin drop turned out to be about a half-mile down the road from their actual house, so I wound up driving up and down the road for about fifteen minutes, trying to find them before we eventually connected on the phone and then continued to talk until we found each other. On the second occasion, I got a pickup request seemingly from Waikiki. Upon arrival at the pickup point, it turned out the rider was at Aloha Tower, which is at least four miles away from Waikiki. I had to cancel that ride and wound up eating the loss. The third occasion happened when I had a pickup request for a girl near the Kaheka neighborhood, but she was actually in Waikiki. Being relatively near enough, I drove to Waikiki to get her, but upon arrival, she was nowhere to be found and was not answering my calls or texts. I assumed her phone had died since she didn't come across over the phone as the type to blow someone off. I wound up eating the loss on that one, which *really* irritated me because I'd wasted about a half-hour trying to find her. Tech support screwed me over too by not agreeing to pay me for my time even though I met the qualifications for a "no show" payout, citing some bullshit line that "I should have canceled the ride at the original pickup point." I'm still irked about that. Cheap bastards.

Pickup in the Middle of the Pacific

Perhaps the most egregious GPS fails are the occasions when it says the pickup locations are offshore in the middle of the Pacific Ocean. This occurs every once in a while, and to my recollection, it has happened to me perhaps three times. Needless to say, each and every time this has happened, I've called the rider to get the actual pickup location.

It would be cool to think, though, that maybe one day, amphibious cars will be built so we can drive to the edge of the water, transform into amphibious mode, and simply drive on water.

CHAPTER 7
"I'M SORRY, OFFICER."

"May I See Your Driver's License, Insurance Card, and Registration, Please?"

It's inevitable. As a rideshare driver, because you are driving on the road more, you have a greater chance of violating a traffic law. And thus, your chances of a traffic stop go up. In the one year that I've been a rideshare driver, I've had way more traffic stops than I had the twenty-two years I've been a licensed driver. It's kinda spooky. Thankfully, the Honolulu Police Department is nothing like the police departments and traffic stops you see all over social media in the "Black Lives Matter" posts.

If all be told, while it sucks to get pulled over and cited, I can honestly say that every officer I've dealt with was professional, courteous, and, ultimately, just doing his job. I will vouch and go to bat for our law enforcement officers as upholding the vows they've taken to enforce the laws of Honolulu with integrity and respect; any media stories of dirty officers are the exception and not the norm. Or at the very least, in my experience, that has been the case. Fortunately, I don't need to deal with police officers that often because I'm a law-abiding citizen who occasionally may make an honest mistake.

Five Miles over the Speed Limit

A few months into my rideshare career, I spent an evening taking fares throughout Honolulu. It was about 10 p.m. in the evening, and I had just done a drop-off in Waikiki and was heading back up Kapahulu, waiting for a new ride request to come in. I drove up Kapahulu the same way I'd driven a thousand times before until I passed a group of cops on the side of the road. They flashed their lights at me and waved me over. "Fuck! Seriously?" I thought to myself. I pulled over and rolled down my window, waiting for the officer to approach.

When he came up to my window, he gestured toward his speed

"I'M SORRY, OFFICER."

gun and asked, "Did you know you were going five miles over the limit?"

"I didn't realize that, officer; my apologies," I replied. Of course, in my mind, I was thinking, *Really? Five miles?* We went through the usual routine of me handing over my license, insurance, and registration, and then he headed back to his vehicle to check me out.

A few minutes later, a younger officer approached to return my stuff and give me a ticket. He thanked me for cooperating and added, "I know five miles may seem silly and trivial, but there have been a lot of pedestrian accidents here lately so we're out here tonight enforcing the speed limit. I do appreciate your pulling over and cooperating with us. A lot of guys will blow us off and we need to track them down later, so thank you for cooperating tonight. As always, you're welcome to write to the judge."

Yes, it sucked getting pulled over and being cited. The fine did wipe out just about everything I had earned that night. And I did write to the judge—I pled guilty since facts are facts and I was going over the speed limit, but I asked for leniency given I was not excessively going over the limit nor driving recklessly.

TALES FROM BEHIND THE WHEEL

I was happy to receive a reduced fine. As for the officers, they were just doing their jobs, so while I was bummed that I was out about a $150 that I really couldn't afford to lose, I do commend our officers for doing their important work with integrity and class. The officers were cool in their interaction with me, so I have no complaints. And I am ever more mindful of the speed limit now whenever I see cops around.

When You Drive on Autopilot While Listening to the GPS

One risk of driving with GPS is becoming an automated slave, simply responding to its orders. Sometimes, the GPS will tell you to turn a little bit earlier than you're supposed to. This can be a problem at night when it's dark and difficult to read street signs. Therefore, GPS was responsible for my second encounter with Honolulu's Finest.

I was going through Chinatown up River Street for a pickup on Pauahi Street when the GPS ordered, "Turn right onto Pauahi Street." Unfortunately, I was about to pass Hotel Street when it called for the turn, but like a Pavlovian dog, I turned right, onto the bus-only Hotel Street. At first, I didn't realize I was on Hotel

"I'M SORRY, OFFICER."

until I noticed there were no other cars; my mind started to think, "This doesn't look like Pauahi." Then I saw a bus in the distance and it clicked for me. "Oh, fuck! I'm on Hotel!"

I drove as quickly as I could to get off the bus-only street, praying a cop wouldn't see me. No such luck. As soon as I rounded the corner onto the next street and tried to ninja away, police sirens sounded and blue lights flashed behind me, pulling me over. I knew I was toast. Same drill and story with the officer who approached, and a few minutes later, the cop came back to return my documents and explain why I was pulled over while handing me my ticket. When I explained the situation, he said I was actually not the first driver to report that, but while he sympathized, he had to maintain the law. He actually recommended that Uber drivers should collectively look into a class action suit against Google for a botched GPS system. Not a bad idea, although to this day, I haven't done so.

My encounter with the officer ended with us wishing each other a good night. Again, it sucked to be basically out of my entire earnings for the night, but once again I wrote to the judge, asking for leniency and received it. So again, I had a positive encounter with Honolulu's Finest—stiff ass fine notwithstanding.

TALES FROM BEHIND THE WHEEL

Driving on the Shoulder of the Road

A few months into my rideshare career, I had a pickup request from deep within the industrial area late at night. I thought to myself, *Who the heck is there at this time of night?* I honestly felt a little creeped out to go there since while I imagined it was some worker getting off *really* late, I also feared it might be something a little less desirable.

I drove twenty minutes to get to the pickup point, only to arrive to an empty gate with no one around. I called and texted, but I got no answer from the passenger. Then, not wanting to lose out on a good ride, I drove around a few minutes, thinking maybe the rider had misplaced the pin. Since it was an empty industrial street, I drove on the shoulder of the road so I could better look for any sign of life. As fate would have it, the telltale siren and blue lights suddenly appeared behind me, and I, once again, found myself needing to pull over.

The cruiser pulled up beside me and the officer rolled down his window. He said, "I want to know why you're driving on the shoulder of the road." I replied, "I'm an Uber driver and I got a pickup request from around here along this gate, so I'm try-

"I'M SORRY, OFFICER."

ing to figure out where my rider is." The officer chuckled and looked amused. Then he said, "Okay." We wished each other a good night and he drove off.

A minute or two later, a huge group of men emerged from beyond the gate. It turned out this was a Coast Guard facility, and the Coast Guardsmen were ready for a night out on the town. We had a fun ride back to Waikiki together, but for the purposes of this particular tale, I'm just glad the officer accepted my story with a laugh and I wasn't forced to take a field sobriety test or anything like that. It helps that I wasn't actually drunk, but when he first saw me driving on the shoulder, he probably thought I was. Overall, another good, respectful encounter with Honolulu's Finest.

"Your Lights Are Off."

One of the dangers of our modern vehicles is our overall reliance on the technology they come with. Both of my cars have "automatic headlights," which turn on and off automatically, depending on the time of day and light conditions. I've come to take it for granted that my lights are *always* on or off when

TALES FROM BEHIND THE WHEEL

I need them to be because I always leave them set on "Automatic."

Occasionally, that is not always true; sometimes, I may bump them, or I may turn them off myself when I pull over to wait for ride requests or if I valet park when going out somewhere. I've had two law enforcement encounters when my lights were off. Occasion number one went by innocently enough. I was cruising down the Ala Wai, waiting for a request to come when a cop pulled up beside me at a stoplight and told me my lights were off. I thanked him, turned them back on, and that was the end of that.

Occasion number two didn't go quite as smoothly. Once again, I was going down the Ala Wai, actually en route to a pickup. I was about four buildings away from the pickup point when the ever-dreaded siren and blue lights flashed behind me. Realizing what the officer was probably pulling me over for, I scrambled to get my lights on, but nonetheless, I pulled over as required. The officer got out of his vehicle, and then we went through the usual song and dance. He warned me about the dangers of driving with my lights off, especially since I would have passengers as an Uber driver. Fortunately, he left it at a lecture and

"I'M SORRY, OFFICER."

warning. Then he returned my license and documents, wished me a good evening, and we both went on our way.

I drove off a few hundred feet to the driveway where I was supposed to pick up my ride. A group of college girls piled into the car and then asked, "Why'd you get pulled over?" I recited the story as I drove them back to their dorm, grateful that my earnings for the night didn't get wiped out and that the officer was merciful this time out. And I think the girls were relieved to know it had been a simple mistake and they weren't riding with a reckless driver or a criminal.

"You Can't Wait Here. You Need to Keep Moving."

One of the biggest challenges with rideshare driving, especially at night, is being cognizant of all the signs on the road regulating things such as "no stops," "no parking," "no turn on red," and various other driving no-nos.

My final encounter with law enforcement my first years as a rideshare driver was due to one of these. I'd gotten a pickup request from a popular Waikiki bar and had pulled up to it. Wouldn't you

TALES FROM BEHIND THE WHEEL

know it—no passenger. Despite several calls and texts, I got no response from the would-be rider. Irked, I resigned myself to waiting out the five-minute wait time to collect my no-show fee.

Since the bar was a popular pickup spot, I'd many times seen various cabs and Uber and Lyft cars swing by to pick up fares and many also pulled over waiting for rides. Since it was still a little early in the evening, it was just me waiting. Other cabs and rideshare cars were lucky simply to pick up their passengers and go. So there I was, waiting uncomfortably as the minutes ticked down. As luck would have it, Honolulu's Finest pulled up behind me while I nervously waited. In the past when I'd swing through there to pick up rides, I would occasionally see a cruiser or two parked there with cops hanging out presumably to help with crowd control since this corner was home to two of the most popular bars in the area. I hoped that was the case this night. However, then I saw the telltale blue light flashing behind me and an officer walking toward me.

"Excuse me, sir; you can't park here," the officer said after I rolled down my window, pointing toward the traffic sign several feet away, which I hadn't noticed earlier. "You'll need to move around the corner or wait elsewhere."

"I'M SORRY, OFFICER."

"Oh, okay. My apologies, officer," I replied as I restarted my car. Then I pulled around the corner as directed to keep waiting for my five minutes to expire. I'd have been really pissed if I had gotten a ticket while waiting for a no-show passenger. Fortunately, the Law Enforcement Gods had showed me mercy yet again.

CHAPTER 8
"I'M HERE. WHERE ARE YOU?"

When They're Not Where They're Supposed to Be

Coupled with GPS failures, there are times when riders simply aren't where they are supposed to be, whether due to a flaky GPS or flaky human error. In this chapter, I'll share some of those tales.

Halloween Havoc

Halloween, by all reports, is one of the busiest nights of the year for rideshare drivers. My first rideshare Halloween was no exception. It was the single most profitable night for me all year. (That would have been different had I driven on New Year's, but oh well).

TALES FROM BEHIND THE WHEEL

One of the funniest things about Halloween is passengers requesting pickups off the side of the road because of the massive crowds of people everywhere.

That night, from the streets of Waikiki to Chinatown, hundreds of costumed partiers all needed rides. The streets were jammed, so it would take quite a while to get to ride requesters. As a driver, due to the length of time it will take for you to arrive, you have to worry that some of these riders will cancel on you.

The funniest parts of the night are when you'll call riders to say, "I'm here," or "I'm just around the corner," but they can't find you because of the crowd, or the riders will call you and say, "We're in the _____ costume," and you look out into the masses. The problem is *everyone* is in costume, and among a literal sea of hundreds, you're not going to be able to tell one cat, nurse, pirate, or cop costume from another, just as the riders aren't going to be able to tell one four-door sedan from another in a stream of a hundred cars inching by without getting into position to read their license plates.

And that was Halloween Year One in a nutshell. Despite the craziness of the worse-than-rush-hour traffic gridlock, it was worth

"I'M HERE. WHERE ARE YOU?"

it to see everyone's awesome costumes, and the beyond-insane surge and primetime pricing paydays made it worthwhile.

"I Walked Over to the Store."

It was a request like any other. I had just dropped off someone in Waikiki when my app pinged almost immediately. *Not bad*, I thought. *Just two streets over*. I pulled out and headed en route. Of course, given Waikiki's penchant for one-way streets, I'd have to go two streets the other way before I could swing back for the pickup.

I did just that, arriving at the pickup point to no passenger on the corner. As usual, I called and texted, but to no answer, and being unable to wait there, I did another lap around the block, still to no one waiting.

After another call, I finally got the female requester to answer. "Oh, sorry!" she said. "I requested it at work, but I walked over to the convenience store to pick up something so I'm here now." Really? Just a little irked but controlling my voice, I replied, "Oh, okay. Where is 'here'? Which store are you at?" It turned out she was at the store on the corner of the street I was originally on after my last drop-off. Shoot me now. I headed back that way and picked her up, thinking, "This would have been nice to have known fifteen minutes ago."

"You Expect Me to Walk Two Blocks?"

Sometimes, people will request rides from areas where you simply *cannot* pick them up. Many major thoroughfares do not allow stops or pickups, or there is nowhere to pull off safely so you need to pick up passengers on a side street. Such was the case one night in Waikiki. It was about 1:00 a.m. when I got a ride request to pick up someone on Kalakaua, where no stops are allowed. Occasionally, you get lucky and find a driveway to pull into, but such was not the case this time around.

When I got to the pickup point, I drove as slowly as possible to see whether I could do a quick pull up to snag my rider since the streets were empty, but there was no way I could wait for a passenger if she wasn't ready. Of course, no one was waiting on the curb for me and there was no driveway to speak of that I could pull into, so I passed by and turned off on the next side street about two blocks down.

"I'M HERE. WHERE ARE YOU?"

I called the passenger after pulling off the road. An angry young woman picked up the phone and began complaining about how quickly I had passed her by. I explained that it was illegal to stop and there was no driveway to pull into (which she disputed). In any event, I offered either to come back around to grab her or she could walk the two blocks to me.

At that point, she bitched, "You expect me to walk two blocks to you?"

I resoundingly replied, "Yes, or I can come back to you." Making passengers walk to a safe pickup point is pretty standard in rideshare driving.

Obviously used to getting her own way, she declared, "I'm just going to cancel and get another driver."

I replied, "That's up to you, but I'm right here ready to grab you. I can come back around for you or you can walk."

Of course, she chose to get another driver. I doubt her experience went any better unless she moved to another pickup point that was safer.

Millennials and their sense of entitlement.

TALES FROM BEHIND THE WHEEL

"Okay, We're Walking Down _____ Street."

Toward the end of my first year as a rideshare driver, I had yet another pickup in Waikiki where either the pin drop was a block off or the GPS took me to the opposite side of the property since the passengers were not on the corner or nowhere nearby. Fortunately, these folks picked up on the first ring, but that didn't help since they were tourists, had no clue where they were, and couldn't read the street signs. I was not overly familiar with this part of Waikiki either, and I was far enough from the street signs that I couldn't read them either. So there we were, idiots on the phone trying to explain where we were. I had to look up my location on the GPS map and read them the street corners I was nearby, but that meant nothing to my tourist friends. Eventually, they started walking until they were close enough to the street corner to see the street signs and pinpoint their location for me. Then I was able to find it on the map, move, and swoop in to their new pickup point.

A frustrating start, but at least they were waiting and ready to go, GPS or human error issues aside. Botched pickup points are always one of the worst parts of rideshare driving.

CHAPTER 9
THE VIRTUAL WATER COOLER

No Coworkers...

When I first started out driving, I found it a very isolating experience. On the one hand, you're with people all day, even if just for five to twenty minute stints. But it wasn't like most jobs where you get to know your colleagues and work alongside them every day for years on end. I had no coworkers to speak of, so for me, it was simply go out and do my thing, and then come home with stories to share with my girlfriend (and my Facebook followers) at the end of a shift.

I enjoyed the freedom of working on my own schedule and at my leisure, plus the constant change of scenery and meeting interesting people from around the globe, but I honestly missed

TALES FROM BEHIND THE WHEEL

the camaraderie of getting to know a group of colleagues and developing a sense of extended family with them like I did all the years I worked in academia. None of that existed for me as a solopreneur—until I found the online driver Facebook groups.

A Community

It turns out that my rideshare feelings of isolation were not an isolated incident (pun very much intended). Many other drivers felt the same way, so to combat this, they turned to social media and formed Facebook groups to meet other drivers. And slowly I found them. My favorite group, of course, happened to be the one for Hawaii drivers—then I had found my tribe. Day in and day out, it became routine to wake up to the group posts, to tune in throughout the day as we shared stories and inside jokes with each other, and to sign out at the end of the night, just like you would in a regular workplace—just virtually.

As with other workplaces, the group's purpose went beyond asking for help and advice with the job and venting about things specific to us like traffic and horrible passengers, or sharing funny moments. A true sense of family developed as

THE VIRTUAL WATER COOLER

we shared personal moments like needing help moving, praying for sick children and spouses, and hanging out together at picnics, the bar, or even each other's homes. We became a community of drivers and an extended family. It has been a pleasure and an honor to share each and every one of our own "Tales from Behind the Wheel" moments with each other over the past year—both the good and the bad. In fact, this book is dedicated just as much to my online rideshare family as it is to the members of my own family who have supported my writing efforts and career.

Thanks, guys.

A FINAL NOTE

"The road of life twists and turns and no two directions are ever the same. Yet our lessons come from the journey, not the destination."

— Don Williams

Thank you so much for staying with me through to the end of *Tales from Behind the Wheel: Year One*!

My hope is that you, too, will choose at some point to create your own "Tales from Behind the Wheel" moments and take up part-time driving for both the laughs as well as the awesome extra-income opportunities that rideshare driving offers.

Through my tales, you've learned some of the basics of how

TALES FROM BEHIND THE WHEEL

ridesharing works. You've learned the benefits, you've learned the pitfalls, and you've learned the frustrations. You got to laugh at some of the strange characters I met. You got to experience the everyday life of a driver. All of these moments are common to most drivers, whether they drive full-time or just a few hours a week at night after their regular jobs or on the weekends.

If you're interested in becoming a driver, I encourage you to do two things:

1. Sign up to drive for either Uber or Lyft, or better yet, both! (Yes, both!) You can use my referral codes below to take advantage of ongoing sign-up bonus specials:

   Uber: Go to Uber.com to sign up or download the Uber Partner app from your App Store or Google Play Store.
   Enter Referral Code: 7avf4qscue
   to be eligible for your new driver bonus.

   Lyft: Go to Lyft.com or download the Lyft app from your App Store or Google Play Store.
   Enter Referral Code: JONATHAN008938

to be eligible for your new driver bonus.

A FINAL NOTE

2. I encourage you to read my companion book *Driving Profits and Making Bank: How to Make Money Ridesharing and Grow Your Business* where I share with you not only how the rideshare business works, but also an overall introduction to how owning your own business works. You also have the option of enrolling in my short online companion course. More information is available at http://www.drivingprofitsandmakingbank.com.

Finally, if you're interested in learning more about ridesharing, please feel free to contact me. My email address is jon@akamaivisionary.com and my cell number is (646)-481-5198. Please email or text me with your name and time zone and I'll be glad to schedule a complimentary consultation with you.

Whether you choose to take up ridesharing and create your own Tales from Behind the Wheel moments or not, I wish you prosperity and happiness in whatever moments you choose to create in your life for yourself and your loved ones.

> "No matter where you are on your journey, that's exactly where you need to be. The next road is always ahead!"
>
> — Oprah Winfrey

TALES FROM BEHIND THE WHEEL

To your continued health, wealth, and happiness.

With Aloha, your friend,

Jonathan K Wong

Jonathan Wong, MBA, M.Ed., MPA

Honolulu, Hawaii

APPENDICES

APPENDIX A

RIDESHARE ETIQUETTE

All drivers have the same frustrations with certain types of riders. Below is a list of what's come to be accepted as proper etiquette for passengers. As a rider, you'll make your driver's life easier, earn better passenger ratings, and not be considered a douche if you can abide by these.

1. **Don't keep your driver waiting.** Drivers are not paid during time en route to pick up points or time while off-trip. Please respect your driver's time and be outside, ready for pickup. Passengers who make their drivers wait at the curb when they arrive do get lower ratings compared to passengers who are outside ready to go.

2. **Don't try to squeeze more people into the car than it can handle.** Most jurisdictions have seatbelt laws or laws regarding car capacity. Sitting on each other's laps or shoving folks in the trunk is dangerous, if not illegal. Request two cars or request an UberXL or Lyft Plus vehicle if you have a big party of people. Do not haggle your driver to squeeze your friends

in. When you squeeze too many people into a vehicle, you screw your driver out of cash since X or Lyft rides pay less than XL or Plus rides. Plus, you put yourself and your driver at risk of a dangerous situation should a car accident occur or law enforcement pull him over for a seatbelt or car capacity violation.

3. **Pick up the phone or reply when your driver tries to call or text.** There's a very good reason your driver is calling. Either he's trying to make sure he's got the right pickup location or you're not where you're expected to be and he's trying to find you.

4. **Do not stand up your driver.** Just like with dates or other appointments, it's extremely rude and uncool to stand up someone and not cancel or return messages. If you no longer need the ride, cancel it right away so you don't waste your driver's time and gas. On your end, you'll also be subject to the "no-show fee." You don't want to pay money you don't need to, so be respectful and smart and cancel right away once you determine you don't need a ride.

APPENDICES

5. **Do not cancel on your driver when he's a good way toward you.** One of the most frustrating things that can happen for a driver is when he has started driving toward you and is more than halfway there when a cancellation notice comes in. Your driver has spent precious time and gas to head your way, braving traffic conditions, so be polite.

6. **Enter the correct pickup address on the app!** Another frustrating thing for a driver is to arrive at a destination only to find out the destination was inputted incorrectly. One of the best things you can do as a passenger is to input the address manually, or if selecting a prefilled destination, ensure that it is the correct address! Sometimes, multiple locations of a franchise business are operating on the same street but a few miles apart and the GPS will select the other location, so pay attention to the address. "Dropping" a pin is not recommended because sometimes the GPS hiccups and the pin goes off by a block or two.

7. **Tips are always appreciated!** Your driver is a service worker. Average base rates may not necessarily cover your driver's costs of time, gas, maintenance, and insurance. Just as with your food server at a restaurant or your barista at Star-

bucks, tips are what help put drivers above the red (unless, of course, you're paying a Surge or Primetime rate, but still, tips are *always* appreciated).

8. **Ask before you change the music station.** Seriously, it's not your car!

9. **Don't leave rubbish behind.** It's the driver's personal car! Just like when visiting a friend's house or a public space, clean up your rubbish or take it with you! Always leave a space as clean as it was when you arrived!

10. **Don't be a dick to your driver.** Show common courtesy. Please be respectful to your driver. Avoid hassling, heckling, or being belligerent to him or her and avoid making inappropriate comments. Some drivers do not put up with shit and will boot you from the car if you don't behave yourself.

APPENDIX B
NEW RIDER OFFER

Let us do the driving!

Not an Uber or Lyft rider yet? Whether you want to enjoy a night out on the town safely (avoid getting a DUI), need a ride to work or school, or a cheap ride while traveling, your friendly neighborhood rideshare drivers will get you there in one piece!

Download the Uber or Lyft apps today.

New riders using the below referral codes will enjoy ride credits toward their first ride(s) free or at a deep discount. Discount offers vary by city.

Uber: Go to Uber.com or download the Uber app from your App Store or Google Play Store.

Enter Referral Code: 7avf4qscue

for your new rider discount.

TALES FROM BEHIND THE WHEEL

Lyft: Go to Lyft.com or download the Lyft app from your App Store or Google Play Store.

Enter Referral Code: JONATHAN008938

for your new rider discount.

Earn additional free/discount rides when you share your referral code with your families and friends!

New Driver Offer

Make your own "Tales from Behind the Wheel" moments.

Whether you need extra money or want to build a new career, become a rideshare driver for Uber or Lyft today!

Download the Uber Partner or Lyft apps today and sign up to drive!

Here are just a few of the benefits of being a rideshare driver:

- **Be Your Own Boss!** Set your own hours and be your own boss!
- **Make More Money Now!** Weekly paychecks with daily

APPENDICES

pay options will keep the cash coming into your pocket! Get out of debt or earn extra money for the vacation or big purchase you're saving for!

- **Make Your Own "Tales from Behind the Wheel" Moments!** You never know who'll get into your car. Every day is a new adventure!

- **Earn Bonuses!** New drivers using the below referral codes will enjoy sign-up bonuses upon completing a minimum number of required rides in a certain time frame! Bonus offers vary by city.

Uber: Go to Uber.com to sign up or download the Uber Partner app from your App Store or Google Play Store.

Enter Referral Code: 7avf4qscue

to be eligible for your new driver bonus.

Lyft: Go to Lyft.com or download the Lyft app from your App Store or Google Play Store.

TALES FROM BEHIND THE WHEEL

Enter Referral Code: JONATHAN008938

to be eligible for your new driver bonus.

To be eligible you'll need the following:

1. A valid driver's license

2. An eligible car (four-door sedan or truck) Year 2000 or newer (some markets 2005 or newer)

3. Vehicle registration

4. Vehicle insurance in your name or as a covered driver

5. Pass a criminal background check

6. A clean driving record

APPENDIX C
DRIVING PROFITS OFFER

Order Jonathan Wong's companion book *Driving Profits and Making Bank* today!

Learn the ins and outs of the rideshare business!

Learn how to boost your profits with business-building strategies!

Learn the basics of running your own business!

Read *Driving Profits and Making Bank* or enroll in Jonathan's Driving Profits course to learn all the tips and secrets of the trade.

The Book

Driving Profits and Making Bank is available at the following locations:

- Directly from Jonathan at www.drivingprofitsand-makingbank.com if you want a personalized copy
- Amazon.com

TALES FROM BEHIND THE WHEEL

- Barnes and Noble
- EBook
- Kindle Store
- Nook Store
- iBooks
- Google Play Store
- Audiobook
- Audible.com

The Course

Boost your learning further by enrolling in Jonathan's "Driving Profits Course" available at www.drivingprofitsandmakingbank.com.

APPENDIX D
TURO OFFER

Share Your Extra Car

If driving is not for you, know that you can also make extra money by renting out your extra car on Turo!

You set the availability!

You set the rates!

Earn extra cash. Weekly paychecks with daily pay options will keep the cash coming into your pocket! Get out of debt or earn extra money for the vacation or big purchase you're saving for!

Rentals are fully insured for theft or damage!

Not comfortable sharing your car? Save on your own rentals when traveling or when your car is in the shop!

Go to Turo.com to sign up or download the Airbnb app from the Apple Store or Google Play Store.

Use referral code: 1409582rDMmlh

for a discount on your first rental.

TALES FROM BEHIND THE WHEEL

Airbnb Offer

Rent Out Your Extra Room!

Make extra money renting out your extra bedrooms or couches in your home! Whether accommodating vacationing tourists, business travelers, or short-term residents, you can earn a great side income or build a thriving business on Airbnb!

Earn extra cash.

Cover your mortgage or rent! Get out of debt! Save for that vacation or big purchase! Fund your child's college education!

Save On Your Own Travels!

Airbnb hosts often offer accommodations at a third of the cost of a hotel or motel! Enjoy the amenities of home!

Go to Airbnb.com to sign up or download the Airbnb app from the App Store or Google Play Store.

Use referral code: JONATHANW72

for a discount off your first rental.

ABOUT THE AUTHOR

Jonathan K. Wong, MBA, M.Ed., MPA is a Honolulu-born and based author, blogger, podcaster, professional speaker, success coach, and organizational consultant. A former college instructor, counselor, technology trainer, instructional designer, and administrative professional of fifteen years besides being a trained and certified Information Technology professional, Jonathan now travels the road teaching success seminars and workshops and delivering keynotes on topics such as academic success and career, business, and leadership development. A Native-Hawaiian professional, he takes special interest in working with indigenous and minority-serving clients and organizations.

Throughout his academic career, Jonathan earned his advanced degrees in business administration, education technology, and public administration, and over the years, he has lent his expertise in technology and business to various individuals and organizations through his Akamai Visionary Consulting practice.

Jonathan's hobbies include studying the martial arts; learning

TALES FROM BEHIND THE WHEEL

about alternative, traditional, and complementary healing styles; playing video games; and watching superhero movies and professional wrestling. He has extensive studies in Chinese kung fu in the Hung Gar and Choy Li Fut styles, Okinawan Karate in the Shorin-Ryu and Uechi Ryu styles, Muay Thai boxing, Brazilian Jiu-Jitsu, and the ancient Hawaiian martial art of Lua. In his alternative and complementary healing studies, he has done extensive study as an energy healer and bodyworker, having certified as a Reiki Master (Usui style) and Pranic Healer, and has studied bodywork modalities, including Thai Massage, Reflexology, Cranial Sacral Therapy, and Hawaiian Lomilomi.

A part-time performance artist, Jonathan is trained in improvisational theatre and as a TV, film, and voice actor. He performed for several years with several Honolulu-based troupes and theatre companies in short form and long form improv. As an actor, he occasionally performs supporting roles in various independent films and web productions, and he provides voice work for various projects.

He is always available for success coaching, organizational consulting, trainings, seminars, workshops, and keynote speaking gigs.

Jonathan resides in Honolulu with his fiancée Liane.

Start Your Small Business Today!

Akamai Visionary Consulting is the small business consulting and coaching practice Jonathan Wong runs to help the everyday person start and grow his or her own small businesses. If you're interested in learning more about ridesharing business opportunities or have other small business dreams, he'll be glad to work with you.

A trained MBA and IT professional, Jonathan offers to you his knowledge of developing businesses plans, marketing plans, risk management, team building, and management and various technology solutions to help you start your business, develop your business, optimize your business, or expand your business.

Visit akamaivisionary.com or call or text (646) 481-5198 or email jon@akamaivisionary.com for consultation rates and packages.

Jonathan Speaks

Entertain * Educate * Engage

As a gifted and prolific speaker and entertainer, Jonathan Wong draws on his years of studies, teaching experience, and performance background to craft a unique presentation for your audience.

A college instructor and trainer of fifteen years with expertise in leadership, academic success skills, business, health and wellness, life balance, and goal setting, Jonathan speaks on various topics of interest to business associations, corporations, and governments.

A performing artist of over a decade, Jonathan is a trained actor, comedian, and musician, having performed on Honolulu's

TALES FROM BEHIND THE WHEEL

improv, sketch, stand-up comedy, and independent film scene for over ten years. Raised in a musical family and having gone on to elective music studies at the high school and college level, today Jonathan is a vocalist, guitarist, and ukulele musician who covers genres ranging from inspirational music to acoustic contemporary. His speaking engagements always hit the mark in terms of educating the audience on the topic while providing an entertaining and engaging experience that incorporates a unique combination of comedic and musical entertainment.

Hire Jonathan today for any of the following:

- Conference keynotes
- Association keynotes
- Corporate trainings
- Government trainings
- Commencement ceremonies
- Business, career, or health fair keynotes
- Youth camps

   Speaking Topics Include:

- Starting-Up for Success

JONATHAN WONG SPEAKS

- Developing Your Inner Leader
- Developing a High Performance Championship Team
- The Superstar Solopreneur
- Building a Hall of Fame Career
- Leading a Balanced Life When It All Needs to Be Done
- Overcoming Depression and Other Mental Illnesses
- Bouncing Back from Failures and Setbacks

To discuss with Jonathan how he can wow your audience and leave it wanting more, contact him at:

http://www.jonathanwongspeaks.com
Phone/Text: (213) 262-9570
Email: jonathanwong.bookings@gmail.com

Succeeding in College and Life

Jonathan's first book, *Succeeding in College and Life*, is targeted toward the incoming college student or college-bound high school junior or senior. Jonathan draws from his fifteen years of teaching and counseling experience working in the community college system and his seventeen-year experience as a college student himself while he completed an associate, bachelor, and three masters degrees.

Some of the topics Jonathan covers in this book include:

- Setting a career direction
- Picking a college major
- Finding the right school
- How to pay for college
- An overview of college support services
- Study skills tips
- Time-management tips
- Money-management tips
- Money-saving and money-making hacks for college students

TALES FROM BEHIND THE WHEEL

- Stress management
- Maintaining a balanced life
- Networking through college to improve your career and job prospects
- How to improve your post-college career and job prospects
- And more!

Visit www.SucceedingInCollegeAndLife.com to order your copy today.

www.ingramcontent.com/pod-product-compliance
Lightning Source LLC
Chambersburg PA
CBHW070807100426
42742CB00012B/2283